The Publicentrist Manifesto

Julius the Jules

Copyright

Revised Edition

Introduction

Publicentrism is a political philosophy that seeks to preserve individual liberty while also bridging the income gap. It is based on the belief that public institutions can be used to promote both of these goals.

Strengthening Public Institutions

Public institutions are the best things that ever happened to the United States. They provide essential services, such as education, healthcare, and infrastructure. They also help to create a level playing field for everyone, regardless of their income or social status.

However, public institutions are under attack. They are being underfunded, privatized, and undermined by special interests. This is a serious threat to our democracy and our way of life.

Publicentrism calls for a renewed commitment to strengthening public institutions. We need to invest in our schools, our hospitals, and our infrastructure. We need to protect them from privatization and special interests.

Socializing the Federal Reserve

The Federal Reserve is the United States' central bank. It is responsible for setting monetary policy and regulating the banking system. However, the Federal Reserve is not a public institution. It is a private corporation, owned by a group of banks.

This means that the Federal Reserve is not accountable to the people. It can make decisions that benefit the

wealthy at the expense of
everyone else.

Publicentrism calls for the Federal Reserve to be socialized. This means that it would be owned by the people, through the government. This would make the Federal Reserve accountable to the people, and it would ensure that monetary policy is made in the best interests of everyone.

Locally Owned Banks Instead

The banking system is another important public institution that is under attack. Banks are being consolidated into a handful of giant corporations.

These corporations are not accountable to the people. They are only interested in making profits for their shareholders.

Publicentrism calls for a return to locally owned banks. These banks would be accountable to the people in their communities.

They would be more likely to lend to small businesses and individuals, and they would be less likely to engage in risky lending practices.

Keep and Strengthen Safety Nets

Safety nets are essential for protecting the most vulnerable members of our society. They provide a financial lifeline for people who are unemployed, disabled, or elderly.

However, safety nets are under attack. They are being cut back, privatized, and made more difficult to access.

Publicentrism calls for a renewed commitment to strengthening safety nets. We need to make sure that everyone has access to the benefits they need to get by.

Preserving Individual Liberty

Publicentrism is not about government control. It is about using the government to protect individual liberty.

We believe that people should be free to do whatever they want, as long as they are not hurting anyone else. We believe that people should be free to own their own property, to control their own bodies, and to make their own decisions about their lives.

The role of government in the economy

Publicentrism believes that the government has a role to play in the economy, but that it should not be the only player. The government should provide essential services, such as education, healthcare, and infrastructure. It should also regulate the economy to prevent monopolies and ensure that everyone has a fair chance to succeed.

However, the government should not interfere in the economy too much. It should not pick winners and losers, and it should not bail out failing businesses. The free market is a powerful force, and it should be allowed to work its magic.

The importance of education and healthcare

Education and healthcare are two of the most important public services. They are essential for ensuring that everyone has the opportunity to succeed in life.

Publicentrism believes that everyone should have access to free public education, from kindergarten to college. We also believe that everyone should have access to affordable healthcare.

We believe that these services are too important to be left to the private sector. The government has a responsibility to provide them to everyone, regardless of their income.

The need for environmental protection

The environment is a public good that we all share. It is our responsibility to protect it for future generations.

Publicentrism believes that the government has a role to play in environmental protection. It should regulate pollution, protect endangered species, and promote sustainable development.

We also believe that individuals have a responsibility to protect the environment. We should all do our part to reduce our carbon footprint and live more sustainably.

The importance of social justice

Social justice is about ensuring that everyone has an equal opportunity to succeed in life. It is about creating a society where everyone is treated with dignity and respect.

Publicentrism believes that the government has a role to play in promoting social justice. It should enforce anti-discrimination laws, provide equal access to education and healthcare, and protect the rights of marginalized groups.

We also believe that individuals have a responsibility to promote social justice. We should all stand up against discrimination and injustice, and work to create a more just society for everyone.

The future of democracy

Democracy is a fragile system. It requires the participation of all citizens to be successful.

Publicentrism believes that we need to do more to strengthen democracy in the United States. We need to make sure that everyone has an equal voice, and that our elections are fair and free.

We also need to educate people about the importance of democracy, and how to participate in it. We need to show them that democracy is not just about voting, but about being engaged in the political process.

Conclusion

Publicentrism is a political philosophy that offers a way to bridge the income gap and preserve individual liberty. It is based on the belief that public institutions can be used to promote both of these goals.

Publicentrism is a new philosophy, but it is based on old ideas. It is based on the idea that the government can be a force for good, and that it can be used to protect the people.

Publicentrism is a hopeful philosophy. It offers a way to create a more just and equitable society.